¡Así debemos ser!
Way to Be!

Ser honesto
Being Honest

por/by Jill Lynn Donahue   ilustrado por/illustrated by Stacey Previn

Nuestro agradecimiento especial a nuestros asesores por su experiencia/
Special thanks to our advisers for their expertise:

Kay Augustine, Directora Nacional y Especialista en Educación del Carácter, Ignite/National
Director and Character Education Specialist, Ignite
West Des Moines, Iowa

Terry Flaherty, PhD, Profesor de inglés/Professor of English
Universidad Estatal de Minnesota, Mankato/Minnesota State University, Mankato

PICTURE WINDOW BOOKS
a capstone imprint

Editor: Shelly Lyons
Translation Services: Strictly Spanish
Designer: Eric Manske
Production Specialist: Sarah Bennett
Art Director: Nathan Gassman
Associate Managing Editor: Christianne Jones
The illustrations in this book were created with acrylics.

Picture Window Books
151 Good Counsel Drive
P.O. Box 669
Mankato, MN 56002-0669
877-845-8392
www.capstonepub.com

All books published by Picture Window Books
are manufactured with paper containing at least 10
percent post-consumer waste.

Library of Congress Cataloging-in-Publication Data
Donahue, Jill L. (Jill Lynn), 1967–
[Being honest. Spanish & English]
Ser honesto / por Jill Lynn Donahue ; ilustrado por Stacey Previn = Being honest /
by Jill Lynn Donahue ; illustrated by Stacey Previn.
p. cm.—(¡Así debemos ser! = Way to be!)
Summary: "Explains many different ways that children can show they are honest—
in both English and Spanish"—Provided by publisher.
Includes index.
ISBN 978-1-4048-6689-8 (library binding)
1. Honesty—Juvenile literature. I. Previn, Stacey. II. Title: Being honest. III. Series.
BJ1533.H7D66 2011
179'.9—dc22   2010040924

Printed in the United States of America in North Mankato, Minnesota.
092010   005933CGS11

Being honest means telling the truth. Even though it may sometimes be hard, telling the truth is the right thing to do. Honest people do not tell lies, cheat, or steal.

Honest people can be trusted.

Ser honesto significa decir la verdad. Aunque a veces parezca difícil, decir la verdad es lo correcto. Las personas honestas no dicen mentiras, no hacen trampa y no roban.

Se puede confiar en las personas honestas.

3

Polly and Patty break a vase while they are playing. Instead of hiding it, Polly shows the vase to her mom.

Polly is being honest.

Polly y Patty quiebran un florero mientras están jugando. En lugar de ocultarlo, Polly le muestra el florero a su mamá.

Polly es honesta.

Tanya's neighbor pays Tanya too much money for feeding the cat. Tanya returns the extra money.

Tanya is being honest.

La vecina de Tanya le paga a Tanya demasiado dinero por alimentar al gato. Tanya le devuelve el dinero adicional.

Tanya es honesta.

Andy finds a purse on his way to school. He takes nothing from the purse. When he gets to school, he gives it to his teacher.

Andy is being honest.

Andy encuentra un bolso de camino a la escuela. Él no toma nada del bolso. Cuando llega a la escuela, se lo entrega a su maestra.

Andy es honesto.

10

Sam's father asks him if he has done his homework. Sam says he hasn't finished it yet.

Sam is being honest.

El papá de Sam le pregunta si ya hizo su tarea. Sam le dice que aún no la ha terminado.

Sam es honesto.

Keesha forgets her brother's new baseball bat at school. Back at home, she tells her brother what she did.

Keesha is being honest.

Keesha olvida el nuevo bate de béisbol de su hermano en la escuela. Cuando vuelve a casa, ella le dice a su hermano lo que hizo.

Keesha es honesta.

During a spelling test, Elliot can see Andre's paper. But Elliot keeps his eyes on his own paper and tries his best.

Elliot is being honest.

Durante un examen de ortografía, Elliot puede ver el examen de Andre. Pero Elliot mantiene la vista en su propio examen y hace su mejor esfuerzo.

Elliot es honesto.

Elliot's teacher makes a mistake on his test score. Elliot shows her the mistake, even though it will lower his grade.

Elliot is being honest.

La maestra de Elliot se equivoca en la calificación de su examen. Elliot le muestra el error, aunque obtendrá una calificación menor.

Elliot es honesto.

While playing hide-and-seek, John runs through his neighbor's garden. John shows his neighbor the flowers and says he is sorry.

John is being honest.

Mientras juega a las escondidillas, John corre por el jardín de su vecino. John le muestra a su vecino las flores y le pide disculpas.

John es honesto.

Jamal and Jem's babysitter asks them what their bedtime is. They tell her the truth.

Jamal and Jem are being honest.

La niñera de Jamal y Jem les pregunta a qué hora se van a la cama. Ellos le dicen la verdad.

Jamal y Jem son honestos.

Ronnie's dad asks what happened to his birthday cake. Ronnie tells her dad that she ate a piece.

Ronnie is being honest.

El papá de Ronnie le pregunta qué sucedió con su pastel de cumpleaños. Ronnie le dice a su papá que ella se comió una rebanada.

Ronnie es honesta.

Internet Sites

FactHound offers a safe, fun way to find Internet sites related to this book. All of the sites on FactHound have been researched by our staff.

Here's all you do:

Visit www.facthound.com

Type in this code: 9781404866898

Super-cool stuff! Check out projects, games and lots more at www.capstonekids.com

Index

Sitios de Internet

FactHound brinda una forma segura y divertida de encontrar sitios de Internet relacionados con este libro. Todos los sitios en FactHound han sido investigados por nuestro personal.

Esto es todo lo que tienes que hacer:

Visita www.facthound.com

Ingresa este código: 9781404866898

¡Algo súper divertido! Hay proyectos, juegos y mucho más en www.capstonekids.com

Índice